THE SPIRIT OF TEAMS

THE SPIRIT OF TEAMS

The Business Leader's Companion to Building Teams

by

Ebenezer Gabriels & Abigail Ebenezer-Gabriels

Explore our BUSINESS Community
at

www.UNPROFANEDPURPOSE.com

Published: September 2022

ISBN: 9781950579648

19644 Club House Road Suite 815

Gaithersburg, Maryland 20886

www.EbenezerGabriels.Org

hello@ebenezergabriels.org

Dedication

TO THE AUTHOR OF TEAMS

FOREWORD

Teams are the pillar of realms - whether nations, communities, families. All people who work together to create a purpose are teams. I am thankful for all the teams I have been a part of, formed, led, and my life's team partner and wife, Abigail Ebenezer-Gabriels.

Abigail is a builder of teams. She has built teams differently and she is a different type of leader than myself. She has called forth the best in people, then I have ever seen any leader do, she has produced the best sales team, and has trained amazing sales leaders.

Ebenezer Gabriels

I love teams. I have built teams and I love being part of teams. I am privileged to be on a family team, and a great team at Ebenezer Gabriels where we are working together to share God's knowledge in us with the world.

Team building skills are a critical need in the journey of a leader. Ebenezer is skilled at putting together highly efficient teams to deliver unbelievable results, and I have watched him build teams from ground zero and deliver extraordinary results, in record time.

Abigail Ebenezer-Gabriels

May the Lord bless you and keep you!

INTRODUCTION

You will need to team up with someone, somewhere someday - whether on a family team or a corporate team. Teams are the core of the organization. The fabric of establishments, and the hands that every leader trusts to bring visions to life.

Teams are the fabrics of successful organizations. Team-building is a core leadership instinct to develop, an art to master, and a skill to practice. The most successful teams are those whose spirits unite with that of their organizations, and fulfill the mission they have been drafted into. Teams can bring visions alive, or bury it - leaders have a definitive edge of molding the spirit of a team.

Spirit of Teams - is the business leader's companion to building teams. Highlighting some of the challenges today's leaders encounter building teams and how to overcome them.

Table of Contents

1

The Soul of a Team

The soul of a team is the barest form of a team, prior to the existence of a team. The soul of a team is formed when a business vision is birthed forth. The soul of a team is the essence that will eventually bind a team together when it forms. The soul being an intangible form of the pillar your organization will need to advance from one milestone to another.

The soul of a team contains the fundamental reasons why the organizational purpose must advance. The spirit of teams hold this important information and individual team members' spirit are all connected to the soul of that team. Once these pillars begin to take its shape, a team spirit is formed, your team's bond runs effectively and fulfills a common purpose.

The team spirit is the life of your team. The team spirit could be positive, negative or neutral. Where a team spirit is positive, the team spirit aligns to the organizational goal, when negative, it does not align, and where neutral, it is neither positive nor negative. Your teams' spirit affects your overall company culture.

A positive team spirit is one of the business most priced intangible assets for sustainability and longevity. All organizations have a unique spirit, and consequently requires teams with matching spirits.

A team spirit reflects in the following way:

- A team buys into a vision. This means a team is united to your organizational goal. The leanings of your team to your organization's goal is sparked by the team spirit.
- Each individual on the team is capable of sharing workload to bring the organization forward.
- Each of the individuals warm up into the team spirit to work with other team members to become one.
- The team begins to work towards one goal, one purpose, and is powered by one spirit.

The team spirit of any company begins with the core HR team - the very one who sits at the top of that ladder. As their spirit is, so the spirits of the organization will be. The HR role in any organization is a highly spiritual role.

The organization shares in the HR spirit, and the remnants of the spirit the HR holds goes across all organizations. HR leaders usually work with the founders of the establishments served, and they are expected to design programs that align with the mission of the organization, as shared by the founder

Where the HR leader goes rogue, they propose anti-mission agendas, which goes against the spirit of the organization itself. Every organization has a key and employee, who is used as the cornerstone of the organization. HR leaders are one of such cornerstones.

There are others who can become the cornerstone of an organization. If your HR person is not solid, or share in the organizational mission, they do not share in your spirit, the people they root for, and the anenda they push goes contrary to yours, hence, your organization spirit becomes diluted, and true cornerstones that can bear the spirit of the organization are missing.

2

Purpose Over Compensation

The spirit of teams is built, not it one day. The spirit of a team is ever connected to the soul of a team. At its finest, individual spirits fuse together with one another, with the organization spirit and unite to one purpose.

Old Functional and Rigid Teams

A functional rigid team is very popular today. This is a team without a spirit, where no bonds exist and everyone comes to do business as usual. On teams like this, the soul of the team is lost, and there is no

Fused Team

There is another type of team, fused team with one spirit is still possible where each team member finds the perfect spot to assume its part in the vision of an organization.

People can get by on a job with compensation, this is not where their truest team spirit is found. created.

When the team spirit prevails, all members of the team thrive. This is where you see people have something to live for.

Team spirit is transferable. Individuals who have worked in a team bond in one organization, when life happens and find themselves in other organizations may still carry the remnant of their former team spirit. You find these individuals giving their best on the job, even without adequate compensation.

Teams like this have the opportunity to change the organization for better. When they arrive on teams, their teams perform better.

Surface-Level

People who do not buy into your visions are there for the pay. They need to use your company to get by. The surface-level romance with your company goes on well for as long as they find you usable. Companies built to last need more than these types of surface-level relationships.

Surface-level employee relations are usually too expensive to manage, emotionally, mentally, and financially.

You will often find yourself paying an employee who is bashing your company, and speaking ill of your company, yet they will refuse to leave, but seek to ruin the hard work of others as long as they are in there, since their spirits do not align in the first place.

It can be very time-consuming to build a strong team spirit. However, it is worth it if founders take their time to bring hiring teams and managers into the core of the vision, to understand the spirits of teams. All organizations have a unique spirit, and consequently requires teams with matching spirits.

2

Hiring Right

Speaking to a founder, she was furious with her employees, it's difficult for them to adapt to digitization, and her company is stuck in the past. She's looking to fire and hire fresh minds.

To fill a team with the right individuals, you need to ensure your base is right. Your base being the right assignments, and tasks, leading and guidance,s the right processes. It's a major disaster if you hire someone into a disjointed process, or into a role without having the right work for them to do.

Organizations are what they are because they run on major processes. Processes ensure results.

Where there are no processes, you will be bringing in people to roam around, without actually reaching the destination you seek. Bringing employees into a role without process leaves employees confused to roam free and most of the time, if they are the very enterprising type, they will create a process for you, one that will drive you nuts.

Many founders do not need one extra employee just yet. This is common in Asia, and this is why there is high efficiency in some of those countries.

Process before Personnel

Do not hire people if you do not know what will occupy their time for the next 8 hours. There is just no point as you will just be burning the fuel unreasonably, something which many startups do.

Hire Problem Solvers

Problem solvers hardly seek to transfer complex issues to others. Hire problem solvers, over non-problems solvers. Problem solvers are built, or have grown to learn to solve problems. Non-problem solvers will shift blame at others at every instance given. They are complainers and complaints are highly contagious, you cannot afford that on a team.

Customer service professionals should be pro problem solvers, yet these could be the most reluctant people to solve a customer problem. Anyone who gives a hint of being hesitant to solve problems will hardly fit into your organization. By doing so, you will be empowering people who will come to sing the problems you hired them to solve into your ears.

Never be afraid of bringing in potential hires for short-term runs to find out what's best. You can both test run for 30-day, or 90 days. However, 90 days is way too long to catch a bad trait. If you have to wait for 90 days, the entire spirit of your team could be endangered.

Never Hire Someone Who Doesn't Know What's On their Resume

Certain candidates are outrightly a bad idea. Don't consider them. It's indeed bad that they scaled through your initial screening. These people are distant from their resume. When you present their resume to them, it looks as though you're speaking a foreign language they do not understand. Some of these people had not read their own resumes because someone else wrote it for them.

Hear Candidates' Pain Points

Abigail was hiring a sales professional for a company. To her surprise, the candidate said, "I do not like rich people, as the rich are not open to a lot of poor people". She ended the interview right there, as the candidate made it easier that they had problems relating with those who could afford the product the company was selling.

3

Exploring Talents

People have different strengths. Not everyone whom you hire into a role will thrive in the role, you may have to adapt some into other roles. You must understand the strength of your people.

It is important for every leader to understand the ability of their team. Leaders are gifted with the ability to search out the gifts in their teams. As a leader, you must look out for hidden gifts in people. People have gifts that have not yet been uncovered or discovered.

If you're a leader searching for solutions on the surface, you will miss out on hidden gifts. People are able to thrive in the face of scarcity and challenges, and this is where gifts come to the surface. During the interview, look for the ruggedness in people, and those who are able to burst into creativity in the face of problems, not people who bluff or boast about everything. Most likely, in the face of problems, they are the first to quit.

An Hiring Leader is an Explorer
As a leader, you are an explorer, and one of your exploring adventures is to search deep into the abilities of your team, whether incoming or current.

What's in this person that I'm yet to discover
What's in this person that I uncovered
What's in them that I cannot figure out yet

Also, humans are prone to change. Leaders should be attentive to the growth of employees by watching for new skills, abilities and professional tendencies. Capacities are released into people for teams' utilization to further an organization's goals.

This is the spirit of your organization at work. Staying attentive to these capacities are the fruits your organization reap for investing in teams. It is abusive to the spirit of your organization when the team's capacities are underutilized.

This is one of the fundamental concepts that birthed forth the HR practice of employee profiling and succession planning. A great HR leader must work with founders to align the organizational spirit to the original vision. When this happens, the organizational spirit is synced, and this becomes a great thriving ground for people.

Teams, when given the optimal opportunity, have the potential to turn every vision into a reality. A team's performance is as good as the belief you have in them, and the vision you instill in them.

4

Spirits Devouring Teams

Starting 2020, a team devouring spirit permeated the media and the airwaves of the United States, and crept into teams across US organizations, fueling the great resignation. News and media outlets began to sponsor the "I quit movement" where many employees "ghosted" their employers.

Employees who had never run a business were deceived into relying on the side hustled economy, while some of them were deceived into warring against their employers. Once a prominent member of a team of 4 was leaving, two would begin making way to leave and it is likely that the one who decides to stay will be asking for a raise. Many American businesses struggled to pull through.

Many startups with low budgets and no funds raised struggled to engage candidates decently on the phone for a preliminary interview as the power had shifted, and the people who once held jobs no longer saw a reason to do so in the resignation-era. This is the spirit of the team at its worst.

Resentments

Resentments in teams break the team's spirit. Resentment, when in the core of a team, will eat the life out of a team, and must be removed. There are two ways to get rid of resentment on a team - the one who carries resentment expels it out when issues are resolved, or they leave with resentment. Either way, resentment is a spirit, and it is the greatest breakthrough when resentment is no longer active in an organization.

Romantic Relationships

Team spirit can be easily broken where romantic relationships build up in a team. Different companies have different policies. When two lovers are on your team, they may team up to deliver the best projects, when their relationship suffers, they are bringing their shattered hearts to wound the team spirit. One of them will get jealous over the other's partnership with another team member, they will step on each other's shoes.

There are couples who met at work, and have built beautiful families. If your organization holds strong family values. The right policies in place can avert any disaster and minimize the risk of romantic relationships. If your organization encourages romantic relationships, it's best you require disclosure and transfer lovers into different departments.

Conflicting Interests

Candidates with conflicting interests should not be brought on the team. These candidates come in with shifty eyes, seeking company resources for personal agenda, or an agenda that benefits their self-interests. Like a fly on a honey, they must not perch on your company's soil. They are desecrating the team's spirit.

Instead, go for candidates who are selfless, with a heart to serve others, with a mind for vision. These candidates still exist. They understand that in the growth of the vision they support is their growth. They are the best team players. They take ownership of the vision of an organization, and are tested hands you can bring into the team.

Leakers

Media's major negative influence has slowly been increasing in the past couple of years and has gotten to a critically alarming level. The role of negative media in team-building is being heightened. The underlying principles to the formation of teams is being attacked by media forces, who have a mastery in slowing down the economic progress of organization by infiltrating teams, dividing and leaking.

Leaking of company's communication has become so lucrative that leakers are seeking to get into your team to steal information to sell to the media. Your company must have a zero-tolerance policy on confidential information.

Negative Media

The role of media in team-building is being heightened. The underlying principles to the formation of strong teams being attacked by the negative media forces, who understand the power of a team, and use its power to stifle economic progress of businesses by misinforming individuals. The negative influence has been increasing in the past couple of years and has gotten to a critically alarming level.

Every modern hiriging executive must understand how the use of negative media affects team building and how to healthily build a team in these times.

Media has promoted cancel culture, a movement that has given birth to entitled employees who when unreasonable demands are not met, take online review sites to discredit employers.

To paraphrase, some news outlets were sponsoring headlines like "how this 19-year quit their 9-5 by working only 20 hours a week and making $1,000,000". Headlines have misled people as not many of these news could be verified. If only a handful of people had success doing this, what's the number of those who were wrongly misinformed. We had younger people showing us the headlines and coming to seek advice if they should quit their 9-5. These individuals who had come for advice had no understanding of what they were looking to do in life. Many of them could not commit to working alone unsupervised for 4 hours, yet they wanted to become self-employed.

A young man went to Thailand on vacation, making ridiculous demands on a hotel, and when his demands were not met, he maliciously dropped a bad review. Being a non-nonsense country, Thailand's authorities investigated and found his review malicious and false. These are the generations groomed by the wrong media influence

To combat the negative influence on false media, it's time to develop in-house media education where you educate employees on sourcing for reliable and true information. Be open about your organization's stand against misinformation. Also be clear to inform your teams of the great advantages and benefits offered by media such as timely information and education. Do not forget to remind them of how destructive negative and malicious media can bring to an establishment or a vision.

Have a healthy relationship with your teams. Have clear communications policies on how issues are resolved. Some employees may not know who to speak to about ongoing issues in your organization. It is important to inform them. Let employees know about non-disparage policies if you have any.

Pay Increases and Counteroffers
People on united teams do not work solely for pay, they work because they share a team bond reflected in the team spirit. When issues of pay increase arise, it is important that your company has a uniform policy. Also, counteroffers are one of the bounce backs that throws off a team spirit. Counteroffers are not always the best decision when a team member is departing. They will always inform someone on the team, and you will have multiple people making ridiculous demands.

Rehires
Rehiring, if mastered, can bring many blessings. The blessing of working with an employee who knows your culture, who shares similar goals, understands your people, knows your processes, and needs little to no training to kick back. Rehiring may also be a bad idea, as things may go back if the one you brought back seeks revenge.

Team Dissolvers

One of the most catastrophic events in an organization is team dissolving characters;

Team dissolving mechanisms could be people:

- Bad hire for an organization
- Good hires gone rouge
- Bad Organizational Policies
- Wrong Communication
- Entitlement Spirits
- Wrong hire for the role

2021 was a terrifying year for a lot of business owners in America, and a lot of employees, about 38 to 40million quit their jobs, for different reasons from low pay to the feeling of being disrespected by employers.

One of the trends amongst employees was discussing their salary, and once there's a significant pay difference observed, employees may ask for more pay or begin looking elsewhere. This was one of the reasons many teams were dissolved, with employees requesting for a raise based on the earnings of their co-workers.

5

Team Onboarding

Onboarding is a powerful tool when deployed right. Onboarding individuals into a team will yield results, positive or negative. An onboarding gotten right will strengthen your team's bond, and bring your team into a higher ground.

In situations where everything goes right, a new addition to a team is supposed to bring your company into a new ground of success, not pull you back 10 steps. Onboarding when done right will achieve the result. When done wrong, onboarding can dilute the flavor of the team, break the spirit of the team, or bring trouble into teams.

Many entrepreneurs lack the team-building skills, hence they will never be able to swerve the critical bends faced by businesses when the need for builders arises. Onboarding alongside training is no small feat, as it requires time, knowledge, and depth into the company. Many companies outsource onboarding and training which is the reasonable thing to do, when your company crosses a certain threshold.

The expertise required for a stranger to train your people and to infuse your business spirit into the hearts of your people is at a different level.

Someone asked Abigail, "despite my busy schedule, is it possible for you to share our company's vision, just the way I have told you to our employees". She answered, "YES". This is what we do with the "Building a Spirit of Organizational Purpose" for teams where founders and leaders authorize and empower us to communicate their visions, and train their employees, bringing them into alignment and unison with organizational purpose. In those workshops or training, we onboard employees into your organization's purpose.

Many organizations drop the ball with their onboarding. You can tell this where an employee does not take up the ownership in their role beyond their daily deliverables. This can only take your company as far as shipping the next product. The place where loyalty exists is the place where employees take utmost ownership of their role in your organization, and are ready to swear by your organization.

In the next chapter, we will discuss the authority of a team, where you will learn how team authority works.

6

Team Alignment

Team alignment is the result of a successful onboarding.

Employees who share your business spirit are those who are internally aligned to your overall business goals. Usually when you hire sales people, sales people who are internally aligned to your revenue forecast share your business spirit and they are ready to go all in.

1. You can observe by looking at how they communicate the value, or seek to find a value to sell to clients
2. You can observe by looking at how they become your customers' advocate, so there is the right product fit.
3. These employees come with the mindset, "while I am here, I would use my talents to advance our company".
4. There is a spirit of ownership and a spirit to get things moving up faster.
5. There is a spirit of problem solving, and a spirit of research, looking to find the right resources to solve problems.

Balanced Strength

Everyone you add to the team must align with the team correctly. Remember, we are all human. Everyone has a strength and a weakness. When there is alignment in your teams, the strength of each one is harnessed, and balance, that the team's strengths combined is potent to deliver the assignment ahead.

The weight of the weakness is not concentrated, as your team is supposed to be like a puzzle that fits into one another. When there is no alignment, you find out that the puzzle does not fit, and there is a visible void.

Employees' Behavior Grieving the Business Spirits

Employees who give a bad impression about your organization to customers do not share the spirit of your business. Oftentimes, where employees say to customers, "My employer is not paying me well", "I hate my job". These are employees who are not honorable to leave, but to hang on the side to get paid but will never share in your business spirit.

Employees who seek to steal from employers. These are the ones never ever sharing business spirits, but hold competitive interests against your business. This is very common amongst sales teams. An insurance company had hired a sales agent full time. The agent was working with another insurance agency part-time as her side hustle. When the agent went to client meetings from the main insurance agency, the agent would knock down her company's product and recommend her side hustle.

There was no way her employer could find out, except that it was difficult to get this employee to send in proper notes from her meetings to the company's CRM. Her notes were never clear, scanty and there were always a lot of excuses why her clients never signed up or purchased an insurance product.

These are major clues that there are no fundamental alignments between an employee and your business spirit. Business spirits are grieved when a business mission rests upon employees who do not share the same spirit.

Where a business spirit is not shared, an employee cannot healthily integrate into a team. If they are, they would break the team spirit.

1. Employees who under deliver and continue to complain about your products.
2. Reporting ethics is poor, and there is no business intelligence whatsoever found in reports
3. Employees who continually get out of processes and procedures

Unfortunately, it is always cheaper to fire them fast, as keeping them could bring your business down faster than trying to reset their minds to fit into your business.

7

The Authority of a Team

A team's authority begins with one individual. This individual catches the raw vision for the existence of business. The authority of a team rests on the one who is most spiritually in tune with the vision given to the team.

A team lead has the authority to lead the team towards a destination. If the one who holds a team authority has any reason to temporarily step aside, out on a sick leave or family emergency, the team spirit leaves on, and that authority remains on the short term with the absent team lead.

Short term absence: Where the leader carrying a team spirit is out for one or two days, the team is self-sustaining, and can deliver effective results, without jeopardizing the spirit of the team.

Mid-term absence: Where there is a mid-term absence which we define as being away from one week or more, authority needs to be temporarily handed over to a strong leader on the team, whom the team can trust, and can hold together the team spirit. Mid-term absence must be watched closely and the right processes must be set in place to ensure that teams do not stray out of processes that have kept the team spirit together in the first place. One of the challenges often associated with mid-term absence is when a team spirit becomes broken.

1. Temporary leader's attention shifts from team focus, to gratifying self.

Long-term absence: Where there is a long-term absence, over one month, there needs to be a replacement leader who carries the team spirit. When this individual is set to depart, there's the need for the authority to be passed on to the next leader, if this process is successful, the spirit of the team is kept intact.

Where the authority of a team is not successfully passed on to another one who is qualified to hold the authority, the one who bears the authority may exit the company. Once this happens, the team may struggle to continue existence.

When an authority is released upon a team, or there is a bearer of a team's authority, the authority conferred empowers the team to go for the goal of the organization, regardless whether the founder is available or not.

BUSINESS BOOKS BY

EBENEZER GABRIELS LEADERSHIP EDUCATION

Ebenezer & Abigail
GABRIELS

The Elements Of

TIME

The Business Leader's Companion to Understanding the Industry of Time

EXPLORE MORE OFFERINGS FROM

EBENEZER GABRIELS LEADERSHIP EDUCATION

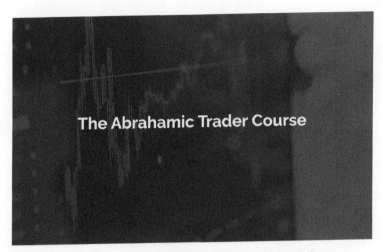

The Abrahamic Trader Course

Abrahamic Trader: Stock Trading - Online 12 Weeks
Delivery Formats: Online, Live, Onsite - and at Client Locations Available

We're in a window in time where God is raising Kingdom Traders to enter into the abrahamic covenant in the marketplace. The Abrahamic Trader Course prepares you to start a business as an Investment Trader, Momentum Trader or a Swing Trader.

The Abrahamic Trader is designed to equip trading leaders with practical, strategic trading to build a steady business in trading. This course is taught based on experiential knowledge and from Biblical and prophetic perspective to equip leaders for the next shift and move in the marketplace. The Abrahamic Trader Course assumes participants have no prior knowledge of trading and prepare traders to gain an edge through sound trading competency development, trading business and management development, and strong risk management and sound judgment and decision making skills.

Africa Business Startup and Expansion Strategy Certificate

African Business Startup and Expansion Strategy Course

Delivery Formats: Online, Live, Onsite - and at Client Locations Available

...

The African Business Startup is a 4-week online course designed to equip you to bring a new business to the continent of Africa. This is the perfect course for those who are looking to tap into the amazing business opportunities in Africa, especially if you are a foreigner called to do business in Africa, or you are an African living in the diaspora. This course aims to equip entrepreneurs and business owners with the information and practical operations on how to build enduring businesses in the African continent.

The African Expansion course is a 4-Week course for existing businesses seeking to expand operations into the African continent and build enduring businesses. The course is designed to help you understand the African business landscape while testing and adapting your business to the AFrican business landscape.

- Develop and learn how best to offer products and services in alignment with the African business landscape
- Learn how to set up an enduring business in Africa
- Learn about unique strategies to thrive in the African business landscape

Why you should get into the course..

- Learn the strategies that Africans in Diaspora can use in running successful businesses in Africa from the diaspora
- Your vision of leading a business in Africa does not have to fade away because others have failed, you need to learn and execute strategies differently.
- Stop relying on friends and families to run a vision they are not built for.

12-Week Software Engineering Immersive Professional Certificate

ithinkicode is for Your High-Schoolers, Recent Graduates and Career Changers

Delivery Formats: Online, Live, Onsite - and at Client Locations Available

...

Become ordained as Software Engineer in 12 weeks. Our programs are designed for you to work on real-life projects from the start, preparing you confidently for incredible earning opportunities and ordaining you as a Software Engineer. Our Software Engineering bootcamp program helps learners acquire on-demand coding and software skills, with hands-on experience, preparing you to serve the Lord as a Software Engineer/Minister of Technology in the marketplace.

Building a Spirit of Organizational Purpose for Teams

Spirit of Organizational Purpose For Teams and Business Executive

Delivery Formats: Online, Live, Onsite - and at Client Locations Available

...

The Organizational Purpose is a 3-day online self-paced course to bring your teams together with a shared sense of unified purpose. This is the perfect course designed to suit your company onboarding needs to bring on new teams and renew visions with existing teams.

The Organizational Purpose course aims to bring new or existing employees into your organizational vision as your organization uncovers the wisdom your team brings, thereby creating a meaningful and mutually rewarding relationship between your organization and teams.

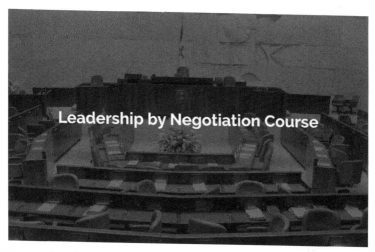

Leadership by Negotiation Course

Leadership by Negotiation Course - 1 Week Online

Delivery Formats: Online, Live, Onsite - and at Client Locations Available

..

The 5-Day Online Self-Paced Leadership by Negotiation is a must for government, corporate and public officials who aim to become sound and influential negotiators. The curriculum provides flexible online learning while completing required course activities onlines.

1. The Negotiation Warfare
2. Negotiation Strategies
   Negotiation and the Mind
3. Imagination and Negotiation
4. Timing and Negotiation
5. The Negotiating Table

Spirit of Salesmanship - Online 4-Weeks
For Sales Teams, Sales Managers and Business Executive
Delivery Formats: Online, Live, Onsite - and at Client Locations Available

...

The Spirit of Salesmanship Leadership training program is designed to develop your team's core internal and external sales instincts and get them prepared to thrive on opportunities to drive your revenue.

The Spirit of Salesmanship Leadership course is designed for sales managers, sales executives, sales leaders. Designed with growth in mind and to sales leaders by fine-tuning and reengineering the mindset and sharpening team, so their sales teams' performance exceeds expectations - while sticking to professional sales standards, deploying the right sales strategy using the right insights and tools for maximum revenue results.

The Career Reinvention Course

Career Reinvention Course - 1 Week
For Career Changers, High schoolers, College Students and College Graduates - Online

...

The Career Reinvention Course is a 7 day on-line intensive program that prepares rising leaders to reinvent their careers, while equipping career changers with on-demands skill sets ahead of time. Learn to build the right framework to stay on top of the industry shifts and maximize income. Our alumni are highly sought after and have landed opportunities in the best-in-class organizations. The Career Reinvention Course brings rising talents to the forefront of their professional undertaking, developing the r providing while equipping career changers with on-demands skill sets ahead of time. Learn to build the right framework to stay on top of the industry shifts and maximize income. Our alumni are highly sought after and have landed opportunities in leading firms including Microsoft and Amazon.

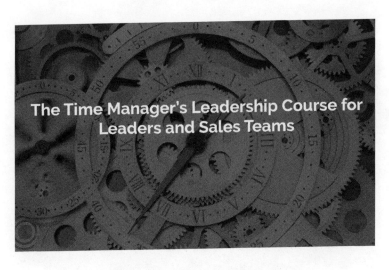

The Time Manager's Leadership Course for Leaders and Sales Teams

...

About the Time Management Leadership Course - Online 4-Weeks - For Teams, Managers and Business Executives
Delivery Formats: Online, Live, Onsite - and at Client Locations Available

The Time Management Leadership course consists of 3 modules and designed to bring leaders and teams into the exploration of the concept of time, and help leaders gain critical time-handling skills, relating with time effectively and developing time management proficiencies.

With the right relationship and mastery of time, combined with time management proficiencies, leaders can stay at the forefront of their goals, aligning people, tasks, activities and results into the right timing. The Time Manager's Intensive Leadership Course is designed to help you acquire on-demand time skills. If you are considering starting a business, or you are an entrepreneur, or a C-suite executive, the Time

Manager's Intensive leadership course imparts you with concise time skills and tools for revenue optimization.

The Spirit of Business Leadership Course

About the Spirit of Business Leadership Course
Online - 8 Week
Delivery Formats: Online, Live, Onsite - and at Client Locations Available

...

Within the next 5 years, business leaders with the right mix of business skills, influence and authority will become the dominant force across all industries. These business leaders hold the secrets of growing dimes and building cents into profitable firms, and will drive positive price and revenue movements by their decisions, whether as an entrepreneur or as a c-level executive. We are ingraining these values in the next business leaders.

The Spirit of Business Leadership is an online and self-paced 8-Week BootCamp Program, designed to shorten your learning curve, while saving you decades. This program is a breakthrough business leadership program, structured to ingrain in you strong and sound business leadership values and education, to lead your firm, operations, technology or revenue growth.

The spirit of business leadership course instills in leaders an unmatched authority to build a product, lead an innovation, or drive sound changes that empowers leaders to bring their firms, or ideas to a stronghold of technological, financial and product advantage.

The spirit of business leadership is a breakthrough business bootcamp designed to launch you into business leadership or scale your business enterprise across generations or effectively lead organizations. During your 8-Week Online Spirit of Business Leadership program, you will explore proven ways to scale products, teams or firms across industries while gaining the agility for innovation.

ABOUT THE AUTHOR: EBENEZER GABRIELS

Ebenezer Gabriels, Founder and President, Ebenezer Gabriels LLC

The President of Ebenezer Gabriels Consulting, Ebenezer Gabriels drives thought leadership for innovation at Ebenezer Gabriels LLC. His 20 years experience in Technology, Innovation, Consulting and Leadership across industries in North America and Asia has earned him the expertise and business acumen that brings sound knowledge and depth to his leadership of all Ebenezer Gabriels consulting projects. He brings deep domain expertise in Technology, Innovation, Platform architecture and Strategy.

Prior to establishing Ebenezer Gabriels LLC, Ebenezer Gabriels has advised business and national leaders, and architected technology, business solutions,and has led several technology teams through different stages of growth across different industries including Fintech, Edtech, Government, Consumer, Banking, Insurance, Emergency Notification System(ENS), Commerce and more.

As CTO, Ebenezer defined strategy for all aspects of technology including performance in the areas of Product Roadmap, Product Delivery, and management, while leading medium to large technology teams effectively.

As a Technology Solutionist for the Singapore Stock Exchange, he led quantitative analysis and data warehousing projects in the Exchange's Business/Derivatives market. As a Senior Architect, he contracted for the United States Department of Homeland Security Customs and Border Control in the R & D unit.

Ebenezer Gabriels consults on Innovation, Data, Technology, Strategy, Finance, Software, E-commerce, Campaign Management, Polls, and more.

He retired before age 35. Ebenezer currently Technology consulting for organizations. He is called to help leaders discover their paths of calling, equip leaders with core skills of their purposes and provide solutions to complex problems in the highest places in leadership.

Ebenezer has brought vast knowledge to the classroom, sharing knowledge and is helping leaders climb higher into their high seat of sound leadership.

Ebenezer Gabriels is a Prophetic Leader, blessed with deep spiritual insights and engages in vision casting for the church, ministry leadership development, church plants, digital ministry transformation, and community development projects bridging the gap between innovation and the church. He brings his prophetic foresight into business visions and long-term strategic planning.

Ebenezer Gabriels received his Bachelor's of Science in Computing (Hons) from the University of Greenwich. When he is not working, he is worshiping and praying, or reading his Bible and spending time with his wife and children. Ebenezer Gabriels spends his free time creating, building new products.

Ebenezer Gabriels is Chief Consultant and Executive Leadership Consultant.

Ebenezer Gabriels' Profile Snapshot

Markets Served:: Asia, US and European markets 20+ Industry Experience

Education: BSc. Computing - University of Greenwich

Core Competencies: Consulting, Forecasting, Government, Insurance, Fintech, Saas, Paas, Iaas, Robotics, Defense Tech, EMNs, E-commerce, InfoSec, Blockchain, Digital Payments, Strategy, Leadership, National Security, Investments, Equity and +++

ABOUT THE AUTHOR: ABIGAIL EBENEZER-GABRIELS

Abigail Ebenezer-Gabriels is the VP and CEO of Ebenezer Gabriels. Abigail advances the goal of innovative and creative consulting, oversees growth, operations and overall success of Ebenezer Gabriels projects.

Abigail Ebenezer-Gabriels is responsible for all marketing, operations, and sales efforts at Ebenezer Gabriels. Abigail brings over 10 years of business, technology, startup and strategy experience to Ebenezer Gabriels. Prior to starting Ebenezer Gabriels LLC, Abigail managed the development and led adoption of various technology products, B2B and B2C across North America, Asia and African markets. She has led the roll out of 3 successful Saas/Tech startups, led more than 20+ enterprise software products, managed multiple online communities and led market expansion into 3 major markets:

In the marketing spectrum, Abigail's proficiencies are startups, market expansion, international markets, digital, branding, content, and strategy. Abigail has also helped launch and grow user base on consumer e-commerce platforms and social media platforms. She has led the design and business efforts to bring enterprise and consumer technology products in industries including hospitality, healthcare, education, industries across different geographies to market.

Her extensive product knowledge spans across various technologies not limited to Business Application Suites, Learning Suites, Media Applications, Security and Emergency Applications, Financial and Banking Apps, Retail Apps, Sales Enablement Solutions, Supply Chain Application Softwares and more.

She consults and educates on a wide array of areas including Strategy, Processes, Policy, Data Analytics, Startups, Software, Financing, Business Design and Modeling, Policy Design, Human Capacity and People Development, Community Development, Education, Communication Design, Strategy, Leadership, Organizational Behavior and Change, Team Dynamics, Opinion Polls, Public Sentiments, Textual Analysis, Sentiment Analysis, Employee Engagement, Social Media Sentiments, Market Research, International Markets, Growth and Strategy.

Abigail Ebenezer-Gabriels is a church leader involved in leadership development, digital church transformation, community development projects and closing the church and innovation gap. Abigail has co-authored 37 books with her husband helping others thrive in their walk with the Lord.

Abigail has successfully led products from ideation to commercialization - advises on policy, security, commercialization. Abigail brings knowledge of product development, strategy commercialization and capital development as a Consultant and the CEO of Ebenezer Gabriels LLC.

Abigail Ebenezer-Gabriels holds a Bachelor's of Science in Marketing from the University of Maryland, Master's of Business Administration, and Master's Degree in Data Analytics. Abigail Gabriels is currently a Public Policy Researcher. Abigail is a wife, mom, and enjoys spending time worshiping with her family, reading and teaching the Word of God.

Abigail Ebenezer- Gabriels' Profile Snapshot

Markets Served: USA & Africa Markets. 8 years Experience .

Education: Bsc. Business/Marketing, MSc. Data Analytics, MBA, Public Policy Researcher

Core Competencies: Marketing, Expansion, Strategy, Education, Human capital and Talent Development, Content, Development,

Operations, Leadership, Product, SAAS, B2B, B2C, Digital, traditional, Startups, National Security, Management -- 4 X Co-Founder and +++

Ebenezer-Gabriels Digital Communities

Ebenezer Gabriels Leadership Education offers top-notch biblically-founded learning experiences through specialized training programs. We create educational contents and deliver in innovative ways through online classrooms, apps, audio, prints to enhance the experience of each audience..

School of Business

www.unprofanedpurpose.com

Marriage Education

www.Blissfulmarriageuniversity.com

Children/Homeschool Education

www.inspiremylittleone.com

School of Ministry

www.IAmUncursed.com

Made in the USA
Middletown, DE
07 October 2022

12104997R10035